Visual IQ Tests

Jola Sigmond

STERLING PUBLISHING CO., INC.
NEW YORK

DEDICATION

To My Ma

The only mother in the world whose two sons both became chairmen of a national Mensa: myself in Sweden and my brother in Hungary.

ACKNOWLEDGMENTS

I express my gratitude to many. Here I wish to mention three by name. For the inspiration: my eldest son Christopher, who ruthlessly pointed out bad features; for the emotions: my former aid Kristina, who contributed to the birth of the book in its early stage; for the will: Rodman, who patiently edited the manuscript into this shape. Without their good will and help I could never have accomplished this book.

I thank several other people, who put obstacles in my way. In reality they have helped me. By lighting up the difficulties I could discover new realms of the mind and thus I can hope to improve my development.

Art Director: Lucy Wilner
Book Designer: Kay Shuckart
Editor: Rodman Pilgrim Neumann

Library of Congress Cataloging-in-Publication Data

Sigmond, Jola, 1943-
  Visual IQ tests/Jola Sigmond.
    p. cm.
  Includes index.
  ISBN 1-4027-0675-8
  1. Intellect--Problems, exercises, etc. 2. Visual perception--Problems, exercises, etc. 3. self-evaluation. 4. Puzzles. I. Title.
BF431.3.S55 2004
153.9'3--dc22   2004009254

10 9 8 7 6 5 4 3 2 1

Published by Sterling Publishing Co., Inc.
387 Park Avenue South, New York, NY 10016
© 2004 by Jola Sigmond
Distributed in Canada by Sterling Publishing
C/o Canadian Manda Group, 165 Dufferin Street
Toronto, Ontario, Canada M6K 3H6
Distributed in Great Britain by Chrysalis Books Group PLC
The Chrysalis Building, Bramley Road, London W10 6SP, England
Distributed in Australia by Capricorn Link (Australia) Pty. Ltd.
P.O. Box 704, Windsor, NSW 2756, Australia

Printed in China

Sterling ISBN 1-4027-0675-8

C O N T E N T S

PREFACE

This book is about *inspirattainment* (inspiration attained through entertainment).

I think that every person is born with very high potential intelligence. Usually this potential is never fully used. As children we imitate others and thus "learn" that it is enough to engage only a tiny part of our abilities. The mechanical education suffocates most of the remaining mind activities and we use a limited part of our potential.

I use the meaning of the expression potential intelligence as all the abilities a human can possess; it includes several kinds. Intelligence can manifest in thinking, e.g., following certain patterns and observing differences and variation; in creating, e.g., using established patterns to deduce the general ideas behind them and discovering similarities; in moving, e.g., applying thinking and creating to physical activities (and I am sure there are some yet-undiscovered abilities, which are dormant in us). And, of course, intelligence is manifest in combining all of these, e.g., in developing senses of rhythm and sounds, shapes, processes; visual imagination, intuition, and imitation.

Using this book one can train and build up certain "muscles of the body of the mind."

The book gives the opportunity to think logically, to see three-dimensionally, to think four-dimensionally, and to use math. It trains—and (if you enter the train) even *entertrains*—forward and backward thinking while at the same time stimulating creativity.

This is a workout for the brain. And the energy that you gain during the exercises you can use for whatever you want! Transform it into happiness, success, creativity, or pleasure.

—Jola Sigmond
Stockholm, Sweden

BEFORE YOU START

This book contains six Visual IQ tests of 16 questions each and one entry question to begin. For fun, I call my questions HAIQUs. The HAIQU is a riddle which challenges your IQ in a playful way. To enjoy the HAIQUs the most, give yourself some time. You don't need a higher education or some degree to solve a HAIQU. You will have a better result if you are in a good mood. Observe the hints! They are indicated in the title of the HAIQU, in the word given for the multiple choices, or in the question itself.

INSTRUCTIONS

My suggestion is not to work on more than one test in one day and to adopt a time limit for each test of one day.

You can evaluate your achievements in each of the six tests. Since there are 16 questions in each of the six tests, you can check yourself against this scoring:

CORRECT ANSWERS	EVALUATION
16–15	Excellent
14–13	Very good
12–10	Good
9–5	Average
4–0	Having a bad day?

The tests are, of course, designed for one person. If you are from a team and solve them together, I suggest that you subtract two points from your test score for every extra person. Maybe one in a million will solve all of the HAIQUs straight away, but everybody can understand all of them while broadening their horizons and giving their mind a workout.

TYPES OF TEST

There are eight types of HAIQUs in this book.

"Odd one out"—amongst five alternatives you are supposed to find the one that differs from the others in some characteristic way. This can sometimes be disputable, but think "all figures have this feature in common except for this one" instead of "the only one which has this feature is this one".

Series—you are supposed to find the next or the missing figure in a sequence. Look for the "movement", the progress.

Relations—"… is to … as … is to …": look for the transformations, recognize the changes of colors, shapes etc.

Volume—You are supposed to compare one or several unfolded shapes with one three-dimensional figure, or several three-dimensional figures with one unfolded.

Matrix—Find the ninth. These are constructed of squares in three rows and three columns. You are supposed to find the one figure that will fit into the empty place. The figures are arranged in a certain way following a logical structure.

Hextrix—Find the seventh. This type of puzzle is my invention. (Tadaa!) They are constructed of hexagons. You are supposed to find the one alternative that will fit into the middle hexagon.

Triangles or Threex—Find the tenth. This type of puzzle is also my invention. (Tam-tataa!) It is constructed of triangles. You are supposed to find the one among five alternatives that will fit into the empty triangle.

Red herring—This is not actually a type, but rather is the "odd one out" amongst the types. Let's just say it could be anything. In all cases: observe the shape, the color, the progressions—sometimes you have to think on another level as well; use the tools available to your mind, e.g., inductive and deductive reasoning, common sense, and a bit of humor. Some of the HAIQUs are easy and some are tricky; several are of the same type but no two are identical.

My suggestion is that you wait on checking the solutions at the end of the book until you have done all the tests. Even a quick glance can tempt you to give up too soon! Pick the best answer from the choices given.

Remember only one test a day—or as the Ancient One said, "one test a day keeps the madness away."

ENTRY QUESTION

TIE

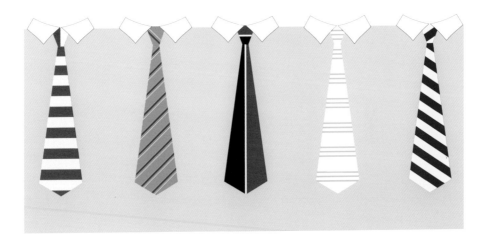

B E G I N

Which tie is <u>not</u> within acceptable limits
to enter the Club?

TEST 1

1. GOING FOR THE ONE

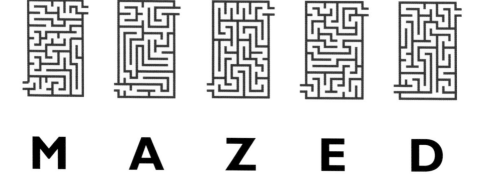

M A Z E D

Which is not reliable?

2. HILL

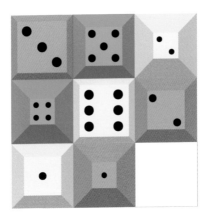

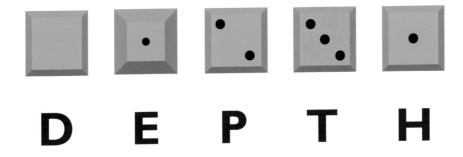

D E P T H

Find the figure for the empty space.

3. IACTA

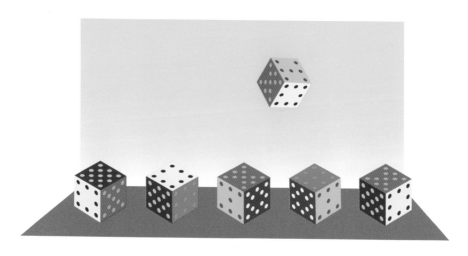

B Y A I R

The die is thrown. Which landing is <u>not</u> possible?

4. TIME BOMB

L A T E R

Watch for the odd one.

5. CAVALCADE

Which figure below should replace the question mark in this sequence?

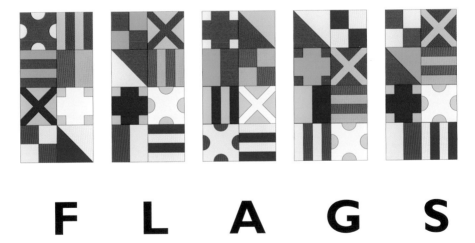

F L A G S

6. MONUMENT

 is to as

is to one of these. Which one?

T **O** **W** **E** **R**

7. LOOM

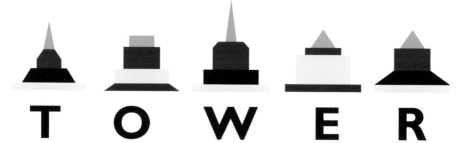

**Which picture below would continue
the row above?**

S **U** **P** **R** **A**

8. MERRY-GO-ROUND

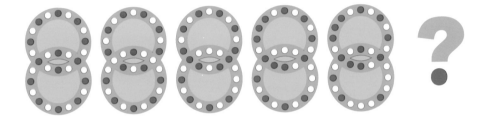

Which one of the figures below
continues the sequence?

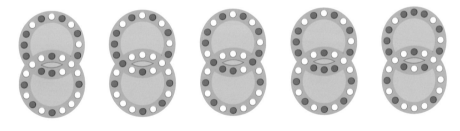

C U R V E

9. ARROW

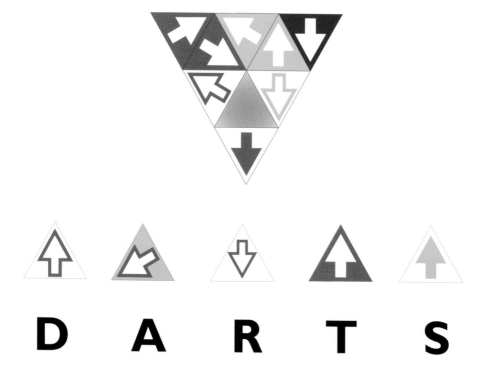

D   A   R   T   S

**Which arrow will fit into
the empty place?**

10. FLAMING STAR

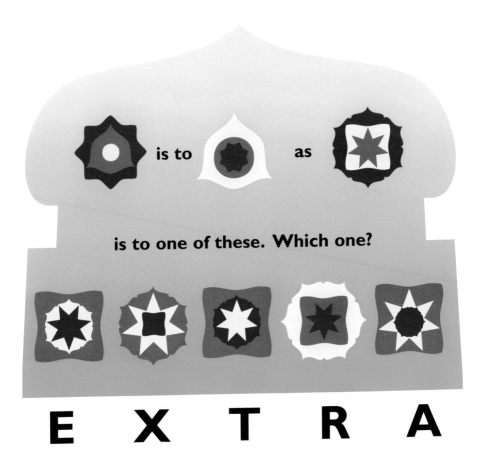

is to ... as ...

is to one of these. Which one?

E X T R A

11. OLD FAITHFUL

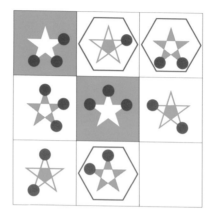

S   **Y**   **N**   **O**   **D**

Decide which option will be at the free space?

12. PARTING THE RED, SEE?

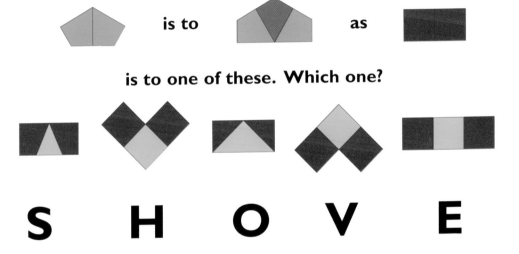

is to   as

is to one of these. Which one?

S   H   O   V   E

13. TIPI

Which building can be constructed from the shape above?

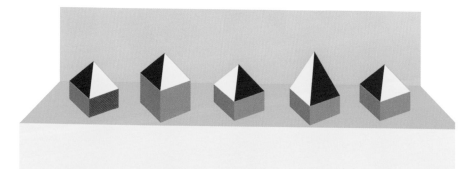

H O U S E

14. HIDDEN

W H I R L

Which figure continues the series?

15. YULE-TIDE

G   I   F   T   S

**Which picture belongs on
the empty place?**

16. RENDERING

M O D E L

Which drawing is the odd one out?

Now you have finished the first Visual IQ Test. Look at it again, explain to yourself why you chose the answers you did, and then have a nice day! Go on with the next test another day!

TEST 2

1. ATOM

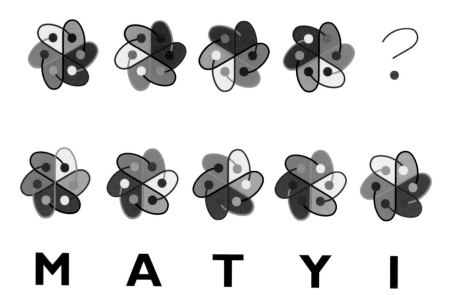

M A T Y I

Which molecule carries on the tendency?

2. TOPOTYPE

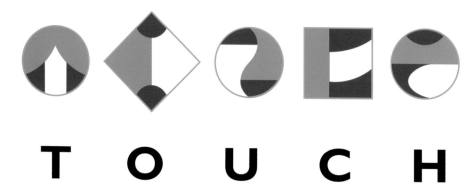

T O U C H

Which figure does <u>not</u> belong with the others?

3. MAYDAY

is to which one of the figures below?

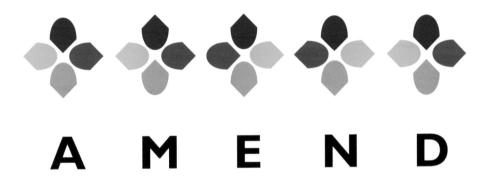

A   M   E   N   D

4. MORE THAN MEETS THE EYE

M A S O N

Which badge has its place in the corner?

5. SUMPLES

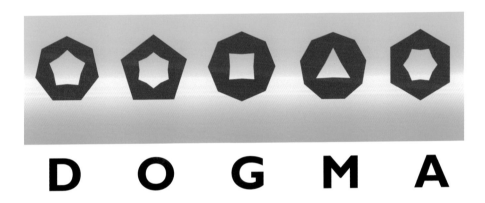

D O G M A

Which fetish belongs to a different belief?

6. TURBINE

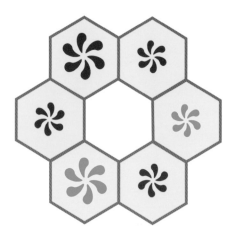

O   R   B   I   T

Which shape will stand in the center court?

7. IT FIGURES

Figure out the next letter.

8. CUBE-A-LIBRE

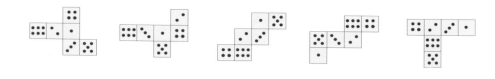

F I X E D

Which one of the unfolded shapes has once been this die?

9. SAP

If is PAT

 is ASP

 is CAT

 is SAC

 is CAP

Which one of these is ACT?

C   H   A   R   T

10. POKER

U N F I T

Find the odd one out.

11. MERGENARY

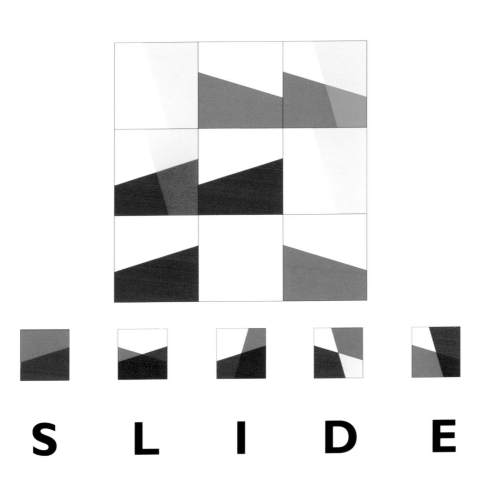

Find the figure for the blank space.

12. BACKVIEW

Here are five pictures of the same die from different angles. Which one of the following figures appears on the indicated side of the fifth picture?

T R A D E

13. STARCASE

 is to as

is to which of the figures below?

N   I   G   H   T

14. MONDRIAN

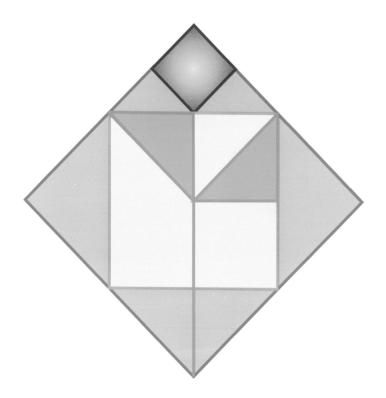

How many squares are there in this picture?

15. CANDLEMATHS

**What numbers are on the next candle
in this sequence?**

16. DINNER

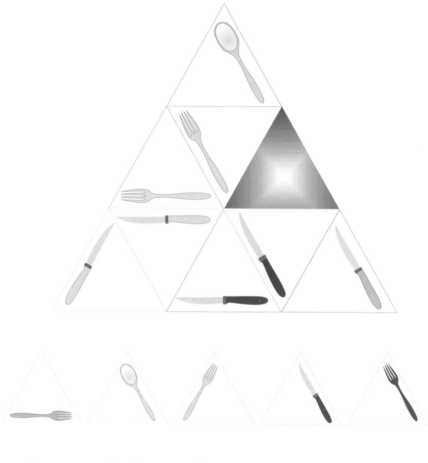

L U N C H

Which piece of cutlery should be served on the remaining place?

So the second test is behind you, fine. Can you notice some progress? Does the mind workout start to show results?

TEST 3

1. JIGSAW

Which one of the pieces below completes the five pieces above?

C   A   R   V   E

2. SILLYNDER

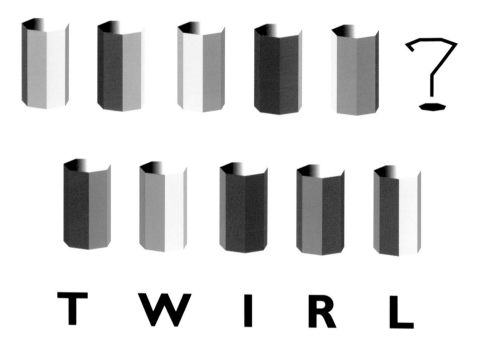

T W I R L

What does the next tube in the sequence look like?

3. ABBA

M A T C H

Which is the odd one out?

4. BOSS

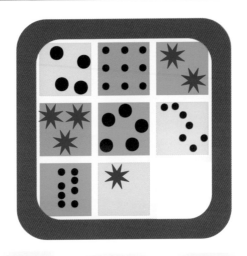

H I N T S

**Which one of the figures should fit into
the empty place?**

5. DAISY

If  is SM

And  is TW

And  is WT

Then what is  ?

F I S H Y

6. DETECTOR

Which one should fit into the unfilled place?

7. XING

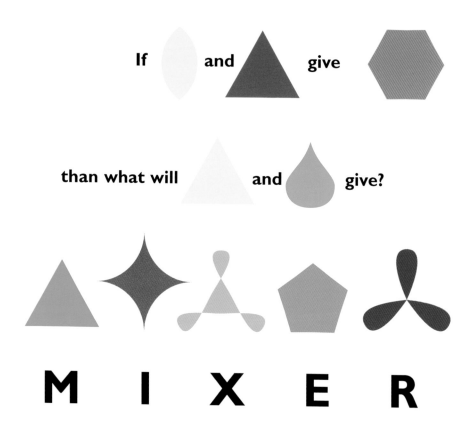

If ⬭ and ▲ give ⬡

than what will ▲ and 💧 give?

M I X E R

8. OCTAHEDRON

Which one of the unfolded figures below can <u>not</u> be assembled into the octahedron above?

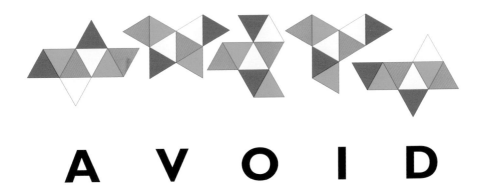

A   V   O   I   D

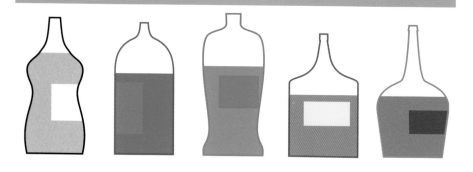

9. BOTTLES

S O B E R

Which bottle is not proper?

10. DEVELOP

5 10 20 40 ? 60

75 80 80 80 90

S T A M P

Which stamp would you glue at the question mark?

11. WRIGHT

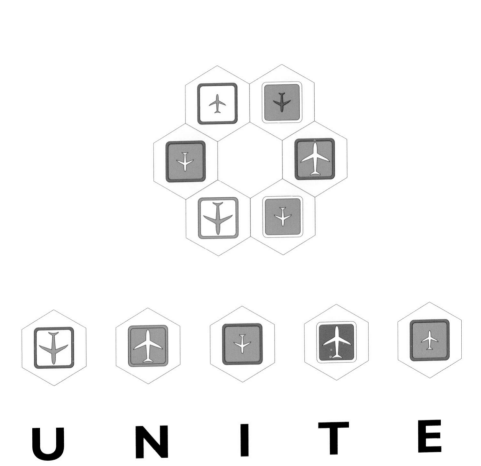

U   N   I   T   E

Which pictogram will fit into the empty place?

12. MAPMAKING

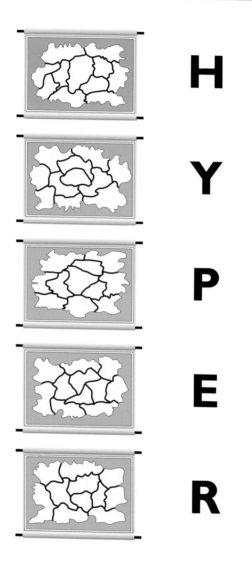

H

Y

P

E

R

Which map is the most colorless?

13. TURNTABLES

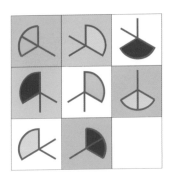

V   O   I   C   E

Which shape will fit into the empty space?

14. FAMILY TEE

T B O N E

The dice family throws a party, with their ancestor's
picture on the wall. One of them, however, brings
her spouse. Which one of the dice comes from
a different family?

15. KALEIDOSCOPE

is to one of these. Which one?

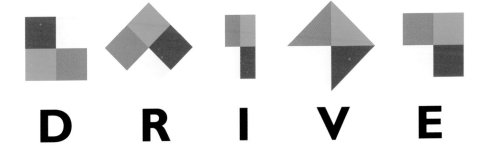

D R I V E

16. ETTER

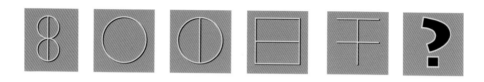

L A U G H

Which code prolongs the sequence?

After the third Visual IQ Test you have probably realized the main types of questions and feel more comfortable about the problem solving. You have come to the half of the whole. Keep the pace that is most convenient for you, but I suggest you wait a day until you go on with the next test.

TEST 4

1. PENTECOST

C R O W N

At the top there is an unfolded die which is colored
on both sides of each square with the same color.
Below there are five dice: four of them are folded
so that the visible sides of the unfolded die are on the
outside. One of them is folded so that the backsides
of the unfolded one are on the outside.
Which die is folded "inside-out"?

2. SEMAPHORE

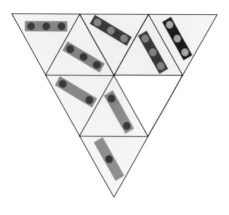

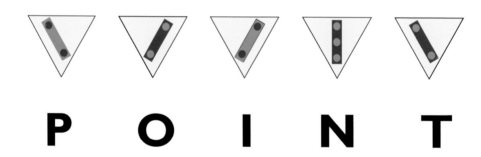

P O I N T

Which figure fits into the empty place?

3. CUT MAN, DO

is to one of the figures below. Which one?

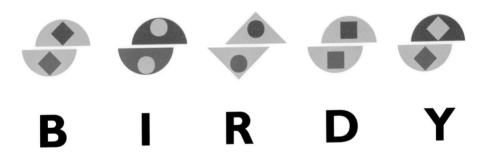

4. FLOORSHOW

T I L E S

What does the missing tile look like?

5. GAMMON

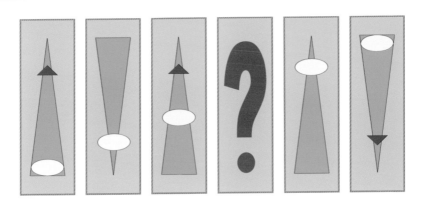

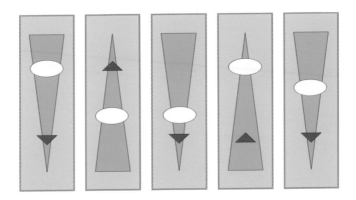

F O U N D

**Which shape will beam up to the place
of the question mark?**

6. FARMOR

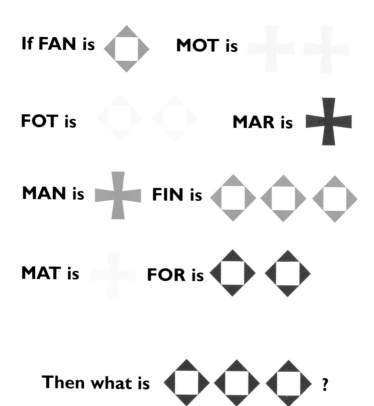

Then what is ◇◇◇ ?

7. THRU

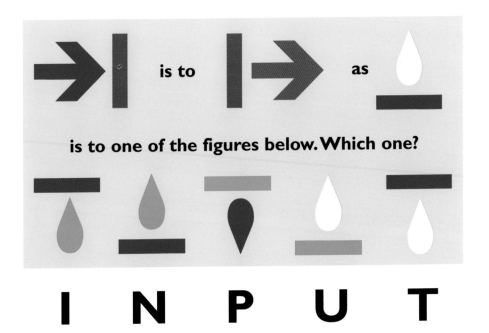

I N P U T

8. EQUAL

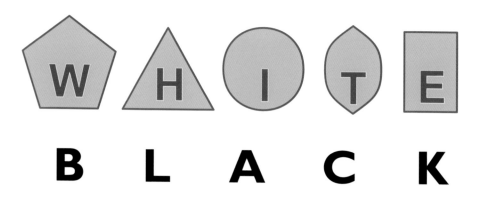

B L A C K

Which figure is the odd one out?

9. BONANZA

Which one of the figures below does <u>not</u> continue the series?

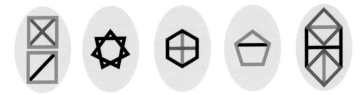

G   R   A   D   E

10. AWARD

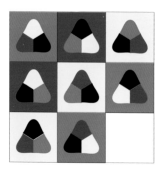

M E D A L

Which icon will suit the vacant location?

11. TECHNO

D A N C E

**Which one of the figures above appears
below front to back (flipped)?**

12. ARTET

Which one of the unfolded figures below can be constructed to form the tetrahedron above?

P   **E**   **T**   **R**   **A**

13. SLY

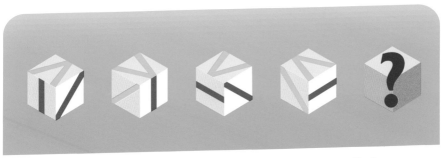

Complete the sequence with one of the
figures below.

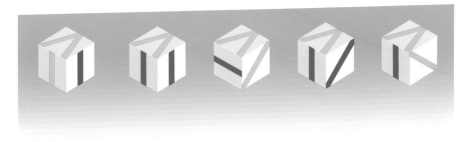

O   T   H   E   R

14. BEMUSE

 is to as

is to which one of the figures below?

R   **E**   **B**   **U**   **S**

15. UMBRELLA

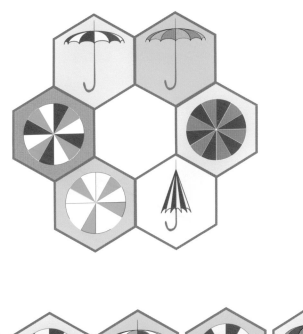

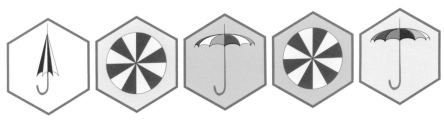

Which umbrella should cover the open spot?

16. ATC

D R A W N

One of the figures is different from the others.
Which?

Now you have finished the fourth Visual IQ Test. Most often you will know when you have found the right answer. Don't go on today and, of course, do not check the answers until after the last test.

TEST 5

1. SURPRIZE

The side of the square is 6 length units. The triangle covers half the square, the square covers three fourths of the triangle.

What is the area of the triangle?

2. MANDARIN

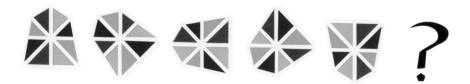

Which one of the following images continues the sequence?

W   I   E   L   D

3. TRIKOTOMI

H E A R T

Which pattern will fill the open space?

4. EWA

C H R I S

Which figure is the odd one out?

5. FLOWER

G R A C E

Which flower will grow in the empty garden?

6. CHERBOURG

What does the umbrella look like from above?

R A I N Y

7. DIALOG

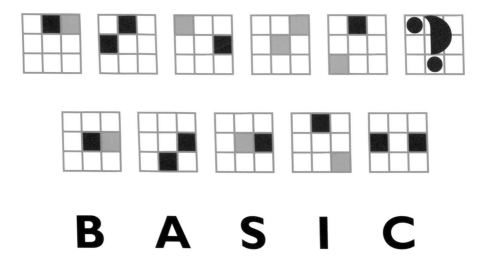

B A S I C

Add the next figure to the sequence.

8. RISING STAR

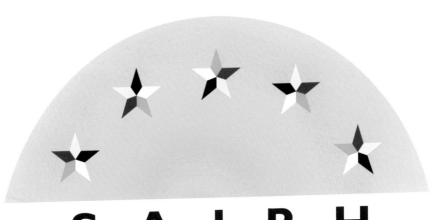

S A I P H

One of the stars above (which one?) should
replaced by one of the stars below (which one?)

R I G E L

9. ZIGZAG

A   M   U   S   E

Find the odd one out.

10. IT'S A SIGN

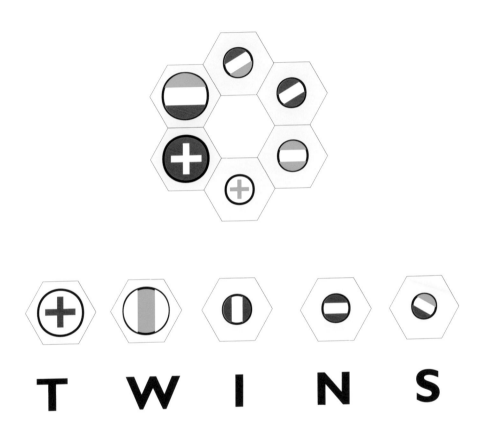

T W I N S

Which symbol should mark the middle?

11. ETALON

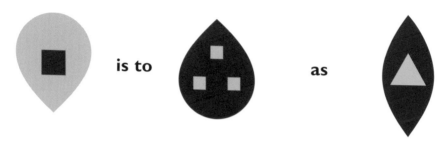

is to

as

is to which one of these?

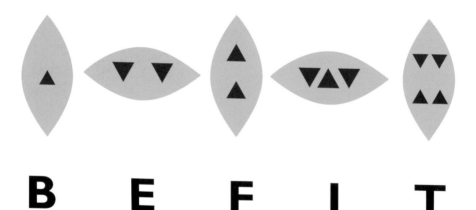

B   **E**   **F**   **I**   **T**

12. MELTING POT

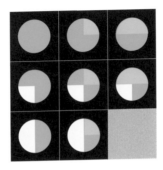

Which figure below fits into the empty space above?

F   A   N   C   Y

13. BENDER

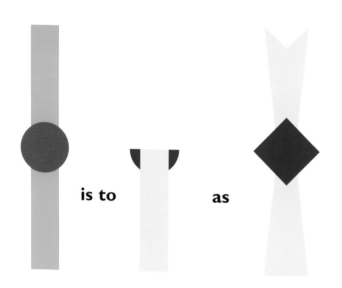

is to   as

is to which one of these?

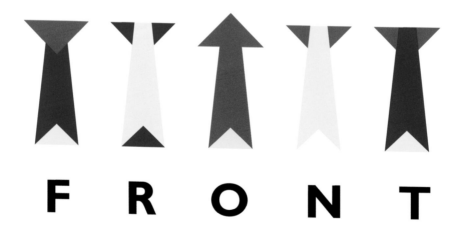

F R O N T

14. ABSID

A B C D E

Which window is appropriate?

15. EYEWITNESS

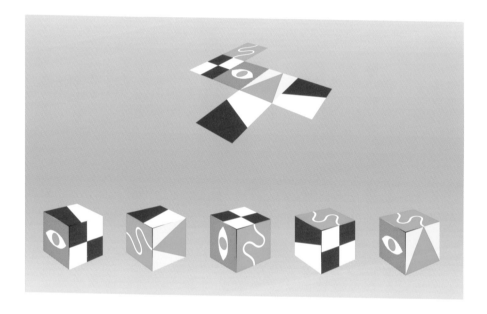

B U I L D

Look for the die that can be folded from the shape in the distance.

16. JAM

is to which one of the figures below?

C R O I X

After the fifth Visual IQ Test you are familiar with the different types of HAIQUs and are therefore prepared for the more tricky ones ahead.

TEST 6

1. ARROWGANTRY

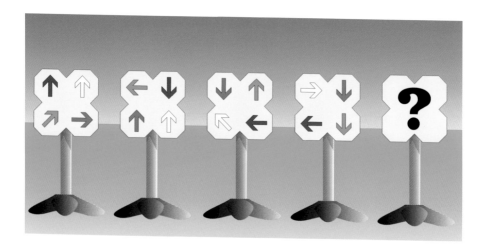

Which shape will be the next in the sequence?

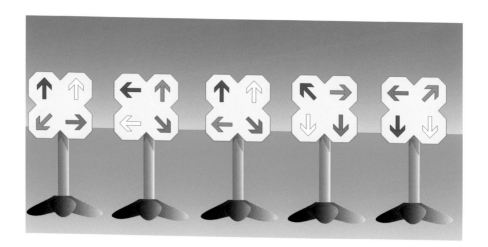

S W I N G

2. PART

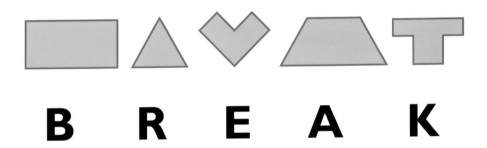

BREAK

Remove the odd piece.

3. TETRA

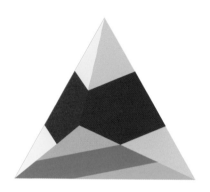

S T U D Y

Which of the unfolded shapes can <u>not</u> be assembled into the tetrahedron?

4. GHOST

S C A R Y

Which ghost will fly in the empty attic?

5. QUACACC

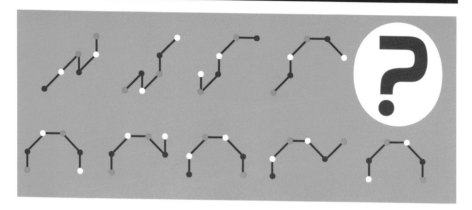

W O R M Y

Which one is the next figure in the series?

6. MARRIAGE

is to ... as ... is to which one of the figures below?

is to which one of the figures below?

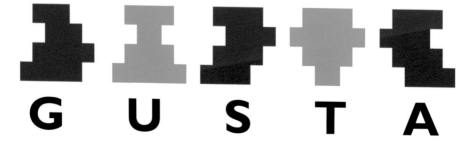

G U S T A

7. NICE DICE

F A K E D

All the dice are nice. One is nice in its own way.
Which one of these cannot be equivalent
to the others?

8. ANIMALS

A L I V E

Which creature can live in the theoretical niche?

9. ENIGMA

ENIGMA

Which one of them is <u>not</u> proper?

10. STOP

is to which one of the figures below?

L O G I C

11. SEENESH

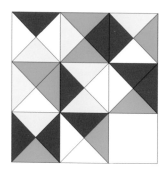

P   A   R   T   Y

Which pattern will fit into the empty place?

12. SKY

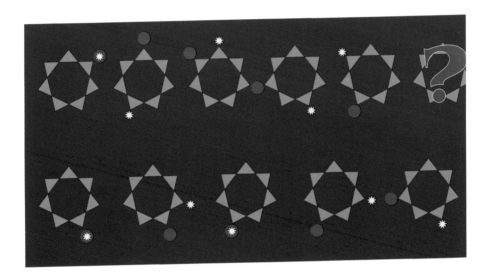

A   S   T   R   O

What is the next constellation in the series?

13. WINDMILL

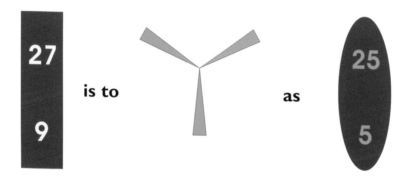

is to which one of the figures below?

T   R   I   C   E

14. BOX

M A G I C

Here is the same die pictured from different angles.
What will the side with the question mark
look like when it is folded up as shown?

15. TRUTH

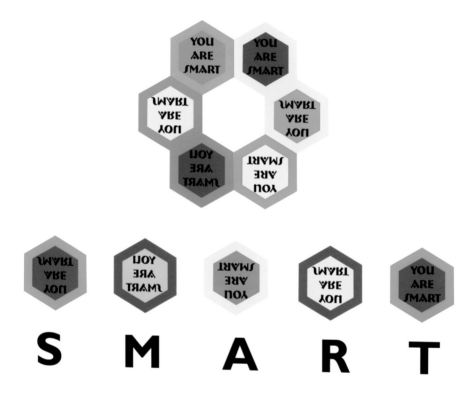

Which of those above is suitable for the center?

16. PYTH-ON

The two red surfaces have equal area. How large is the blue region compared to the green one?

One third of the size	Half	Two thirds the size	Equal	One and a half times the size
A	**D**	**I**	**E**	**U**

So you have arrived at the Moment of Truth. I hope you have had fun during the mind-exercises and that, when you compare the given answers with those of your own, you will increase and reinforce your understanding.

ANSWERS

Entry Question

TIE

I

The other ties follow a certain pattern. On the I-tie the pattern is horizontal even on the knot, which is usually impossible for a tie.

I. GOING FOR THE ONE

Z

All the labyrinths have one way through, except the third, in which there are two different ways to go.

2. HILL

D

In each row and in each column there is one pink, one green and one yellow figure.

In each row and column there is one "low," one "middle," and one "high" figure.

The number of eyes: row one + row three = row two.

Column one + column three = column two.

3. IACTA

A

4. TIME BOMB

A

The others can be the time on a digital watch.

A however, cannot, since there is never a 6 at the third place of a digital display.

5. CAVALCADE

S

The colors move through the figures counterclockwise, one step at a time; the patterns move 1, 2, 3, and 4 steps clockwise.

6. MONUMENT

W

7. LOOM

P

There are all in all three colors, and each picture contains two of them, one on top of the other:

On top: G   B   R   G   R
On bottom: R   G   G   B   B

The only combination missing is blue on top of red.

8. MERRY-GO-ROUND

E

The top and bottom circle rotate one at a time clockwise.

First the upper circle turns one step, then the lower one turns two steps, then the upper turns three steps, etc.

9. ARROW

D

The rows give the attributes of the arrows (blank, with edges and filled),
The /columns give the directions of the arrows,
And the \columns give the colors.

10. FLAMING STAR

A

There are three colors and three shapes.
Shapes: the innermost goes to the middle, the outermost goes to the innermost position (turns a bit), the middle one goes to the outermost position.
Colors: the middle position keeps its color, the outermost and the innermost exchange colors.

11. OLD FAITHFUL

Y

In each row and column there is a white star on a green background, a green star on a white background, and a white star with a green middle on a white background. Of the red dots, two or none appear on a point of the stars in each row and column.

12. PARTING THE RED, SEE

V

Part the first figure into two similar shapes until the space between them gives room to a third equivalent figure and then turn the trio upside down.

13. TIPI

U

14. HIDDEN

W

The two triangles rotate 60 degrees clockwise in every step. The green and red stripes move clockwise and counter-clockwise respectively around the figure.

15. YULE-TIDE

S

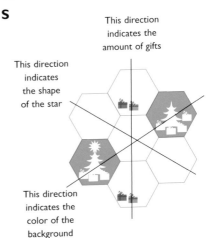

This direction indicates the amount of gifts

This direction indicates the shape of the star

This direction indicates the color of the background

16. RENDERING

L

The others have five separate areas, while in L there are six.

1. ATOM

Y

The large colored areas rotate counter-clockwise one step, the small particles rotate clockwise one step.

2. TOPOTYPE

H

All the figures are divided into four parts. In four of them, two parts are touching all three others, whereas the two others are touching two others. In the fifth figure, one of the parts touches all three others, two touch two others, and the last one is touching only one other part.

3. MAYDAY

M

The four-part figures are mirrored from the center except for the bottom part, which remains unchanged.

4. MORE THAN MEETS THE EYE

A

In each row and column there is a square, a cross, and three small circles.

The colors are: red on white circle, white on red circle, and transparent on white circle. In the case of the transparent "color," the background color is visible through the pattern. The background colors follow the system: one blue, one yellow, one blue, one yellow, etc.

5. SUMPLES

O

For all the other figures the sums of the inner and outer corners are 12; for O it is less.

6. TURBINE

I

The \ direction gives the color (red), the horizontal direction gives the size (small), and the / direction gives the rotation (clockwise).

7. IT FIGURES

T

These letters correspond to the first six numbers, where the name of the number includes the letter at this place in the alphabet:

The word "fivE" contains E, the fifth letter in the alphabet;

"eigHt" contains H, the eighth letter in the alphabet;

"nIne" contains I, the ninth letter in the alphabet;

"tweLve" contains L, the twelfth letter in the alphabet;

"fourteeN" contains N, the four-teenth letter in the alphabet; Finally "Twenty" contains T, the twen-tieth letter in the alphabet.

8. CUBE-A-LIBRE
X

9. SAP
R

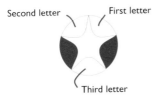

The colors correspond to letters as follows: Blue=P; Red=A; Yellow=S; Green=C; Black=T.

10. POKER
U
In U there are two identical figures among the three. In the other pictures all the figures differ in shape and/or color.

11. MERGENARY
L
In each row and in each column, two of the figures are added to create the third.
The overlapping area gets the mixed color of the two.

12. BACKVIEW
E

13. STARCASE
I
The picture is mirrored and the colors, interchanged.

14. MONDRIAN
6

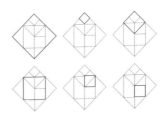

15. CANDLEMATHS
891
The numbers above and below make up the squares of the middle numbers, e.g. $16=4^2$.

16. DINNER

H

The rows give the types of cutlery, the \ columns give the positions and the / columns give the colors:

SPOON

FORK

KNIFE

1. JIGSAW

V

The "tongues" of the jigsaw pieces are inwards or outwards. There are six possible combinations:

4 out 0 in

3 out 1 in

2 out 2 in (two different ones)

1 out 3 in

0 out 4 in

V makes the set complete.

2. SILLYNDER

I

The cylinder rotates around its axis: one step to the right, then two steps to the left, three steps to the right, four steps to the left, and finally five steps to the right.

3. ABBA

C

On the rest, the small figures are the halves of the large.

4. BOSS

I

In each row and each column the background colors are green, blue and turquoise. The missing color is turquoise.

In each row and each column there is one picture containing big circles, small circles or stars, respectively. The missing figure is big circles.

The sum of small circles, big circles and stars, respectively, in each row and column is 15.

5. DAISY

F

The positions in the circle represent the days of the week, Monday through Sunday. The letters are the initial letter of each day.

6. DETECTOR

V

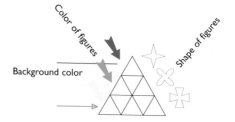

The rows indicate the colors of the backgrounds, the / directions the types of crosses, and the \ directions the colors of the crosses. When a cross and a background are of the same color, the cross will not show.

7. XING

M

Yellow and red mix to orange; yellow and blue mix to green. The multiples of the numbers of corners give the new numbers of corners.

8. OCTAHEDRON

O

9. BOTTLES

O

The color of the bottle + the color of the sign give the color of the liquid.

Black + white = grey

Green + blue = turquoise

Red + yellow = orange

Blue + red = purple

But purple + turquoise does not give green.

10. DEVELOP

M

The prices of the stamps double in each step—this gives the price 80. The background color follows the spectrum backwards—this gives the color orange.

The motifs show a development towards more and more advanced life forms. Gorilla is a primate and fits in between bear and human in this sequence.

11. WRIGHT

I

The \ direction gives the size, the horizontal direction gives the colors, and the / direction gives flying direction.

12. MAPMAKING

Y

All the other maps are possible to color with three colors, and no neighboring lands will have the same colors. On Y however there is a need for four colors to achieve the same demand; thereby most colorless.

13. TURNTABLES

V

Each square contains two overlapping figures:

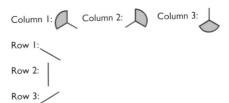

Every column and every row has one of each background color and one of each shade of blue inside the shape. Each square contains two overlapping figures which move through their separate sequences.

14. FAMILY TEE
E

All the others can be folded from the unfolded die on top.

15. KALEIDOSCOPE
E

The small black shape in the middle suggests the shape of the new figure. The colors change places as shown below:

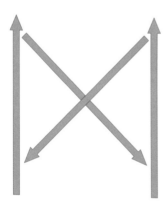

16. ETTER
A

Alternating left and right, the shapes are the mirror images of all capital letters B through G.

TEST 4 ANSWERS
1. PENTECOST
O

2. SEMAPHORE
T

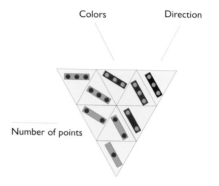

3. CUT MAN, DO
B

Both the inner and the outer figures divide into two figures.

The inner figure becomes the outer, and takes the colors of the former outer figure, so that the color of the border becomes inner color and the inner color becomes the color of the border.

The outer figure parts into two smaller but similar shapes; the color parts divide into their respective component colors: orange becomes red and yellow, purple becomes red and blue.

4. FLOORSHOW

I

The crossing-point moves downwards in the rows and to the right in the columns.

5. GAMMON

D

The green triangle is alternately pointing up and down.
The yellow oval moves upwards one "step" at a time; the small red triangle is attached to the green triangle and sometimes the yellow oval covers it.

6. FARMOR

FIR

The shape indicates the first letter: square for F and cross for M.
The number of shapes gives the second letter: 1=A, 2=O, 3=I. The color provides the third letter: yellow=T, blue=N, red=R.

7. THRU

I

The arrow passes through the rod and changes its color to the mixed color of the arrow and the rod. Similarly, the drop passes through the rod and mixes its color with the color of the rod.

8. EQUAL

B

The other letters are surrounded by figures consisting of the same amount of lines as the letters are made of:
H: triangle—three lines
I: circle—one line
T: "twosider"—two lines
E: rectangle–four lines

9. BONANZA

D

This series is based on the Fibonacci series (1, 1, 2, 3, 5, 8, 13, 21…): the next number is the sum of the two previous.
The color bars represent:
Red=1
Blue=2
Black=3
The sum in G, R, A, and E is 21, while in D it is less.

10. AWARD

E

In each row and column there are three background colors.

The black area is found in all possible positions in each row and in each column: top, left, and right.

Within each of the three of the background colors, the figures rotate one step counterclockwise from the upper row downwards.

11. TECHNO
E

12. ARTET
T

13. SLY
E

This sequence is not a rotating die as one might think at first glance, but three independent, interconnected rhombi.

In each step the "V" in the top green rhombus rotates 90 degrees clockwise, the line in the lower left pink rhombus turns 45 degrees clockwise and shifts colors between red and blue, whereas the line in the lower right yellow rhombus turns 45 degrees counterclockwise.

14. BEMUSE
B

The outer figure turns 45 degrees and takes the color of the inner figure; at the same time it duplicates innermost and keeps its color. The inner figure turns upside down and become white.

15. UMBRELLA
K

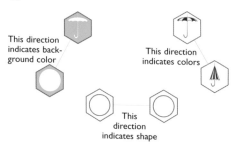

This direction indicates background color

This direction indicates colors

This direction indicates shape

16. ATC
R

The other figures can be drawn in one movement without lifting the pen.

TEST 5 ANSWERS

1. SURPRIZE
24

The area of the square is 36 length units (l.u.).

If the area of the triangle is X, we get the equation:

$$3/4 \ X \ = \ 36/2$$

to which the solution is

$$X \ = \ 24.$$

2. MANDARIN
W

For each step the image rotates 45 degrees counterclockwise and the colors rotate 45 degrees clockwise.

3. TRIKOTOMI

R

The rows give the background colors and the number of figures.

The / columns give the colors of the figures.

And the \ columns give the shape of the figures.

4. EWA

R

5. FLOWER

A

There is one flower of each color in each row and each column. The sum of the petals in each row and each column is 15. The sum of the leaves in each row and in each column is 12.

6. CHERBOURG

N

7. DIALOG

C

Number the squares as on a phone, i.e.,

first row: 1 2 3,

second row: 4 5 6,

third row: 7 8 9.

The sums of the marked squares give 5, 6, 7, 8, 9—C gives 10.

The odd numbers are blue, the even numbers are red.

8. RISING STAR

PL

The first three stars and the fifth above can be turned into each other. The fourth, however cannot. This star should therefore be replaced by the fifth star in the bottom row.

9. ZIGZAG

U

Each figure has 10 corners, of which 7 are convex and 3 are concave. In U, however, 6 are convex and 4 concave.

10. IT'S A SIGN

N

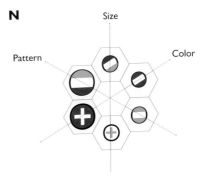

11. ETALON

F

The large figure turns upside down and takes the color of the small one. The small figure divides into a number of even smaller figures, which inherit the color from the original large figure. The number of these small figures is one less than the number of sides of the original small figure.

12. MELTING POT

F

The green fields do not exist, but appear as an overlapping of the yellow and blue.

The yellow fields look like this in each row:

The blue fields look like this in each column:

13. BENDER

T

The figures bend forwards and downwards. The backsides of the shapes have different colors than the front.

14. ABSID

D

The colors, downwards, are in alphabetical order.

15. EYEWITNESS

D

16. JAM

R

The figures are put on top of each other, and switch colors with each other. The areas covered by both figures become white.

TEST 6 ANSWERS

1. ARROWGANTRY

S

The colors move clockwise relative to the positions, disregarding the directions of the arrows.

Each arrow turns counterclockwise at its own regular interval.

2. PART

K

The others can be divided into four smaller shapes similar to the large one.

3. TETRA

U

4. GHOST

S

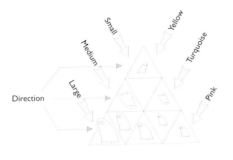

5. QUACACC

W

The color sequence moves 1, 2, 3, and 4 (four being the same as one) steps forwards. The color sequence moves relative to its previous position, disregarding the movements of the worm. For each step one piece disappears at the end (left) and a new one appears at the beginning (right). The new piece turns 45 degrees clockwise from the position of the previously placed piece.

6. MARRIAGE

G

The left (blue and green) figure turns upside down, moves to the right side of the red figure, and takes its color.

7. NICE DICE

K

All the dice can be turned to each other's positions but the green. (Naturally this provides that all of the dice are "nice," i.e. that the sums of the eyes on opposite faces are 7.)

8. ANIMALS

I

In each row and each column there is one of each background color: red (dawn), blue (noon) and violet (dusk) as well as one of each animal color: yellow, brown, and red. In the first column there are birds, in the second mammals, and in the third, extinct animals.

9. ENIGMA

N

Each letter has the same amount of spots as its place in the alphabet. N, however, is the 14th letter but has only 11 spots.

10. STOP

L

The two figures inside the large figure build a shape between each other. This shape takes the color of the two figures in the middle and turns clockwise 45 degrees.

11. SEENESH

Y

Each square has four parts: "N," "E," "S," and "W."
N has colors red, blue, and yellow—one in each row and in each column;

E has colors white, red, and blue—
one in each row and in each column;
S has colors yellow, blue, and white—
one in each row and in each column.
W has colors white, yellow, and red—
one in each row and in each column.

12. SKY
O

13. WINDMILL
R

Divide the upper number by the
lower—this gives the number of
petals. The color is a mix of the color
of the numbers and the background.

14. BOX
G

15. TRUTH
S

The \ direction gives the border color,
the horizontal direction indicates the
text direction, and the / direction
gives background color.

16. PYTH-ON
E

The white triangle in the middle has a
right angle. According to Pythagoras
the sum of the squares of the sides
equals the square of the hypotenuse.
So the red and green areas together
have the same area as the blue square
(including the red circle). If the red
circle—equal to the red triangle—is
removed, the remaining blue area is
equal to the green.

INDEX

A B O U T   T H E   A U T H O R

Jola Sigmond was born in Hungary in 1943. He escaped the Communist-ruled dictatorship on an adventurous journey without a passport and started a new life in Sweden in 1967. He studied at the University of Lund in Sweden and majored in architecture, with further study in the fields of mathe-matics, programming, art history, and psy-chology. He was the secretary of Mensa Nord and then the chairman of Mensa Sverige as well as the honorary president of Mensa Hungariqa.

Being known as "Scandinavia's Most Intelligent Man," Jola (pronounced [yoo-lah]) over the years has constructed a great many tests. These tests are not only IQ-related, but also related to creativity, personality, and ability, and they are regularly published in Swedish, Norwegian, Irish, American, and Hungarian papers. In addition Jola has made several television appearances on Swedish, Norwegian, and Hungarian TV channels.

Jola Sigmond is researching human creativity, and applies his discoveries for practical use in everyday life. He is also an appreciated lecturer, speaking at universities as well as for companies in Sweden, Norway, Hungary, Germany, and Poland. The main focus of his teaching is how to develop the hidden possibilities of individ-uals and organizations.

In his spare time Jola enjoys playing backgammon, seeing films, and connecting with people over the Internet. There are several chat rooms in which Jola directs the conversations, for the enjoyment and pleasure of many.

Jola Sigmond currently lives in Stockholm, Sweden; his website is www.sigmond.se.